...BURY COLLEGE OF ARTS & TEC...
...H COLLEGE CAMPUS

Telephone (01746) 764431 Ex...

Ren...
... stamped.   038

KT-514-543

Radbrook LRC

What do we mean by human rights?

Equal Rights

Maureen O'Connor

W
FRANKLIN WATTS
NEW YORK • LONDON • SYDNEY

This edition 2000

First published in 1997
by Franklin Watts
96 Leonard Street, London
EC2A 4RH

Franklin Watts Australia
14 Mars Road
Lane Cove
NSW 2066

© Franklin Watts 1997

Editor: Helen Lanz
Series editor: Rachel Cooke
Art Director: Robert Walster
Designer: Simon Borrough
Picture research: Sue Mennell
Consultant: Dan Jones of Amnesty
International

A CIP catalogue record for this book
is available from the British Library.

ISBN 0 7496 2605 4 (hbk)
ISBN 0 7496 3825 7 (pbk)

Dewey Classification 323.5

Printed in Italy

Acknowledgements:

Anne Frank, *The Diary of Anne
Frank*, Longman's Encyclopedia,
Microsoft Encarta; Steve Biko, Donald
Woods, *Biko,* Paddington Press,
1978; East Timor, Amnesty
International information; Tuzla,
Bosnia, *The Daily Telegraph*, 11
September 1996; Sweden, Swedish
Ministry of Health and Social Affairs;
Emily Davison, *Chronicle of the 20th
Century*, Longman; Kabul,
Afghanistan, *The Independent*,
9 October 1996; Kuwait, *The
Independent*, 30 September 1996;
London, *The Guardian Weekend*,
10 August 1996.

Picture credits:

Cover image and contents page:
Hutchison Library (Sarah Errington)

Amnesty International (UK) 18B, 20B;
Mary Evans Picture Library 31B; Sally
and Richard Greenhill 22T, 27T, 38
Hulton Getty Collection 9B, 33;
Magnum Photos 10T (Bruno Barbey),
14B (Danny Lyon), 24C (Danny
Lyon), 25R (Thomas Hoepker), 28T
(Danny Lyon), 28B (Chris Steele-
Perkins), 29 (Burt Glinn), 35 (Abbas),
36BL (Patrick Zachmann), 37B
Abbas); Mansell Collection 32T
Network 21T (Jenny Matthews), 34B
(Mike Abrahams); Panos Pictures 14T
(David Reed), 20T (Howard J.
Davies), 22B (Trygve Bolstad), 36T
(Liba Taylor); Photofusion 7T (Sam
Scott-Hunter), 10-11 (Crispin
Hughes); Popperfoto 9T, 11T, 15T &
BR, 16T & B, 17T & B, 18T, 19, 21B,
25L, 26TL, BL & R, 30B, 31T, 32B,
37TR, 39, 42T & B; Rex Features 6B,
7B, 8T, 13tT& B, 24T & B, 27B, 30T,
34T, 36BR, 40, 41TL, TR & B, 43
David Simon 8B, 23; Topham 6T
(Associated Press), 12, 15BL
(Press Association).

SHREWSBURY COLLEGE LIBRARY
INV. No. 020852   DATE 101002
ORD. No. 12916   DATE 20802
ACC. No. 038390
323
PRICE 5-99   CHECKED

CONTENTS

SHREWSBURY COLLEGE
BRIDGNORTH LRC

BEING DIFFERENT

Date: 1991
Place: Iraq
The issue: Being discriminated against for being different

In 1991 the whole world was shocked to see hundreds of thousands of Kurdish refugees trying to cross the bleak and mountainous border between Iraq and Turkey. Men, women and children fled on foot with whatever belongings they could carry. They were trying to escape the anger of the Iraqi dictator Saddam Hussein and his army.

'safe havens'

The Kurds are an ancient people with their own language and culture, but without a country of their own. At least 25 million Kurds live as minority communities across a mountainous region of the Middle East, split between six different nations. As an ethnic minority in each of these countries they have been discriminated against because of their stong cultural identity which they have preserved. For over 70 years some have fought for a homeland where they can speak their own language and observe their own traditions. In 1991, Kurds in northern Iraq staged an armed uprising against the harsh rule of Saddam and his government. More than 1.5 million Kurdish refugees fled as Saddam reacted angrily, sending in troops to crush the protest.

Saddam Hussein's military rule in Iraq since 1979 has been especially hard on the Kurdish minority in the north of the country. But other minority groups, such as the Marsh Arabs in the south, have also been persecuted.

The United Nations tried to protect the Kurds by setting up 'safe havens', zones within Iraqi territory which the Iraqi military were to be prevented from entering. But the havens did not turn out to be very safe. In 1996, Iraqi troops attacked Kurdish towns again. Many Kurds remain in refugee camps with little hope for the future. A secure homeland for the Kurds still seems as far away as ever.

Thousands died in Suleimaniya, northern Iraq, when Kurdish villages were attacked with poison gas, a weapon which is banned under international law.

An equal chance

There is nothing new about the persecution of people who find that they are living where they are not liked or trusted. Just as a bigger child can bully a smaller one in school, so a bigger group of people can treat a smaller group, or minority, unfairly because they do not like their religion, their language or their way of life. That dislike is called prejudice. Treating people unfairly because they are different is called discrimination. Prejudice and discrimination have caused human misery and death on an enormous scale in the lifetime of many people.

There may always be differences between communities and peoples, in income and in lifestyles between individuals and between countries, but we do not have to accept that these differences justify the persecution of people. We can help make the world a fairer place by opposing prejudice and discrimination.

(Above) Who is being bullied in your playground? Is it someone who looks different from you? (Left) In the United States, the Amish people live peacefully with their neighbours although they have a different religion and way of life.

We all dislike some people some of the time. That is human nature. It only becomes dangerous when we dislike people because of things they either cannot change or should not be asked to change: the colour of their skin, the way they worship God or the way people of their culture live their lives. These are aspects that should not alter how someone is treated or the rights that they have.

Time:
1944
Place:
Amsterdam, the
Netherlands
The issue:
How prejudice
can kill

Towards the end of the Second World War a fifteen-year-old girl called Anne-Frank was arrested with her family by German soldiers in the Dutch city of Amsterdam. Less than a year later Anne died in the terrible concentration camp at Belsen, leaving behind her a diary which she kept during the time she had been in hiding from the Nazis. Her diary told how she and her family had lived in great hardship in secret rooms provided by sympathetic Dutch friends until they were finally betrayed.

(Left) The house in Amsterdam where Anne Frank (above) and her family hid from the Nazis has been turned into a museum in her memory. It aims to remind visitors of the terrible results of racial intolerance.

No escape from persecution

The worst persecution of a minority this century was by the Nazi government in Germany, which was in power from 1933 to 1945. The Nazis hated the millions of Jewish people who lived in Germany and the other countries of Europe which Germany occupied after the outbreak of the Second World War. The Nazi government blamed the Jewish community for Germany's economic difficulties. The Nazi leader, Adolf Hitler, systematically set about turning the country against the Jewish community – marking them out as being different because of their race and religion. The Nazis planned the extermination of all the Jews in Europe.

Protecting human rights

After the mass murder of millions of people by the Nazis, known as the Holocaust, the United Nations was formed. This was an organization of 51 countries, whose aim was to prevent such atrocities from ever happening again in a bid to achieve world cooperation and peace. In 1948 the UN agreed the Universal Declaration of Human Rights, a document that set out to ensure that every human being should be able to live in peace and freedom regardless of race, religion, gender, wealth or any such difference.

'basic rights'

The General Assembly of the United Nations brings together representatives of 189 nations to discuss the world's problems.

Can we make life fair?

The Universal Declaration of Human Rights is important because it sets out the basic rights which would enable everyone to live free and equal lives. It condemns the sort of discrimination and persecution which led to the death of Anne Frank and the persecution of the Kurds, and many other groups all over the world today. The Universal Declaration of Human Rights upholds that everyone should have equal rights – that is that they should be treated equally no matter who they are.

Many died in the Nazi concentration camps during the Second World War. At the end of the war there were some 300,000 survivors, including these prisoners at Buchenwald.

(Above) Many countries have minority groups who are treated badly. Romanians often dislike the large Rom (Gypsy) minority. Many of this group find it hard to make a living in an unfriendly society.

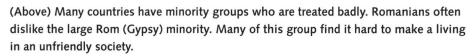

'All human beings are born free and equal'

These are the main clauses of the Universal Declaration of Human Rights that are concerned with equal rights:

Article 1
All human beings are born free and equal in dignity and rights. They are endowed with reason and conscience and should act towards one another in a spirit of brotherhood.

Article 2
Everyone is entitled to the rights and freedoms set forth in this Declaration, without distinction of any kind, such as race, colour, sex, language, religion, political or other opinion, national or social origin, property, birth or other status.

Article 3
Everyone has the right to life, liberty and security of person.

Article 6
All are equal before the law and are entitled without any discrimination to equal protection of the law.

Article 21
Everyone has the right to take part in the government of his country, directly or through freely chosen representatives.

Article 25
Everyone has the right to a standard of living adequate for the health and well-being of himself and his family, including food, clothing, housing and medical care and necessary social services, and the right to security in the event of unemployment, sickness, disability, widowhood, old age or other lack of livelihood in circumstances beyond his control.

What has all this to do with me?

It is not only governments or powerful people who violate, or take away, other people's rights. A nation might persecute thousands of its own people who are in some way different from the majority. But individuals, too, can also take away the rights of others. It happens in little ways, in our schools and colleges, at work, or just in our street.

We all show prejudice every time we let our dislike or fear of an individual or a group lead us to say or do things which are unfair. It is when we act on our dislikes that such prejudice becomes dangerous – when we will not let people who are different join the group in the playground; when we insult them or bully them or allow them to be insulted or bullied without making a fuss.

Power and fear

The more power people have over others they dislike or fear, the more easily they can turn from bullying to discrimination and to persecution. In the worst cases, this can lead to murder. The Universal Declaration of Human Rights is a set of clear human rights standards for governments to follow in order

'from bullying to discrimination'

to prevent discrimination and persecution. Although the UDHR is not a set of laws, each government is expected to follow the standards it sets. Sometimes governments may fail to meet them all, such as the right to an adequate standard of living which may be difficult to fulfil in a world where there is still

Being different

(Above) Groups, such as Orthodox Jews, have a strong visual identity that is important to their religion or culture. These groups often find themselves targeted by other members of society who persecute people who choose to look different.

a great deal of poverty. But it is better to have standards which are sometimes ignored than to have no standards at all.

If the Holocaust showed the worst that human beings are capable of, the Universal Declaration shows the best – it gives us an ideal to aim for in our treatment of one another.

The fact that we are all different is something to be celebrated. When prejudice is driven out, friendships can flourish (below).

FREE AND EQUAL?

Date: 1971 – 1977
Place: South Africa
The Issue: Fighting for equal rights and equal treatment

Stephen Biko was an ambitious black boy who studied hard to get to university in a country where the best education was reserved for white people. He was studying medicine but became so interested in politics and so involved in opposition to the whites-only government of South Africa that he was expelled from his college.

At this time, South Africa was governed by a system of apartheid – the separate development of the races with white minority rule. This meant that the smaller white population held all the power, wealth and rights. Biko led a group of young Africans who were against this system. They believed that black people should stop relying on their white friends for support against apartheid and should help themselves. Biko set up the Black Consciousness Movement to encourage black social and cultural development.

'severely beaten'

The Movement influenced the uprising by black schoolchildren in many of the townships of South Africa in 1976 and 1977, during which hundreds of students were killed by the police and army.

In 1977, Black Consciousness groups were banned by the government. In August that year, Biko was arrested, not for the first time, and so severely beaten by the police that he lapsed into a coma and died. An inquest into his death decided that the police were not to blame, stating that Biko had battered his own head against the cell wall and killed himself.

Twenty years after Steve Biko's death, when a new multi-racial South Africa had at last been established, five of the white policemen involved in Biko's arrest confessed to his killing.

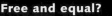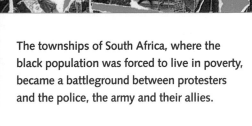
The townships of South Africa, where the black population was forced to live in poverty, became a battleground between protesters and the police, the army and their allies.

A divided country

The government of any country has a responsibility to try to uphold the laws of the country to ensure everyone's well-being and security. But if the people who are in government and control the army and the police force choose to use their power to make laws which discriminate against you, it is very difficult to fight back. Steve Biko fought against the power and injustices of the South African state and paid with his life.

Until very recently South Africa denied its black inhabitants, the majority of the population, basic human rights in their own country. The system of apartheid divided the country by law into a small, privileged elite of white people and the rest. The black population could not choose where to live, what jobs to do, or whom to marry. They were not allowed to vote and so could not vote to change the government of their own country.

Holding on to power

The reasons why countries discriminate against and sometimes persecute groups of their own people are complex. They very often have deep roots in a country's history. They involve powerful emotions of fear and greed, and hatred of the group which is being picked on. They usually involve one group's wish to keep control of government for themselves.

Under apartheid white families earned, on average, 12 times the income of black families in South Africa. One out of every two black workers was unemployed.

A wealthy minority

In South Africa, the powerful and wealthy white minority introduced apartheid as a way of keeping the wealth of the country for themselves. The best of everything was reserved for the white population. There were whites-only schools, buses, hospitals and even parks and beaches. Increasingly, the government tried to make the different racial groups as separate as possible. They fiercely resisted a democratic system of government, where everyone is allowed to vote for a chosen person to represent them in parliament. The whites knew that would mean they would be ruled by the black African majority who would reform the country and try to make blacks and whites more equal.

'determination to end a huge injustice'

Like the Germans before them, the white South Africans created a system of government which resulted in human misery on a vast scale. Nazi Germany was defeated in a world war. But in South Africa change eventually came peacefully, brought about by the whole world's determination to end a huge injustice.

(Above) In 1994, life for white people in South Africa was very comfortable: making up only 13% of the population, they owned 61% of the wealth.
(Below) Even within recent history, black communities have often been denied access to many facilities.

PRIVATE POOL
MEMBERS ONLY

The world outraged

Many countries and individuals outside South Africa were outraged at the use of apartheid. In 1964, the United Nations Security Council condemned what was happening and began to investigate the possibility of economic sanctions against South Africa: governments would stop the buying or selling of goods which were important to the wealth and stability of the country.

By the mid-1980s the United States and the European Union had stepped up their sanctions. Many countries made it difficult, if not impossible, for companies to trade with South Africa.

(Below) South African cricketers celebrate their victory over England after the sports boycott was lifted in 1994.

Sanctions and ordinary people

But it was not only governments which took action against apartheid. Ordinary people all round the world played their part by refusing to buy South African wine and fruit. Actors and musicians refused to perform there, and sporting links were cut. The sports-mad South Africans were particularly upset when other countries refused to play their international teams at cricket and rugby.

(Above) Colby Chandler, the then chairman of Kodak, the photography suppliers, announces a ban on supplying Kodak products to South Africa in 1986.

Eventually, after persistent pressure, the situation in South Africa began to change. After difficult negotiations, the last white president, F W de Klerk, and the leader of the main black opposition party, Nelson Mandela, signed an agreement in November 1993 to establish a new democratic republic on the basis of 'one person one vote'. The first free elections in the country's history were held in April 1994, giving the African National Congress (ANC) a clear victory. It is probably not an exaggeration to say that the whole world rejoiced.

Celebrations as a delighted Nelson Mandela is inaugurated as South Africa's President, in May 1994, with F W de Klerk as one of his Deputy Presidents.

Date:
May 1994
Place:
South Africa
The Issue:
Building a free
and equal
society

Just three years after the last of the apartheid laws were withdrawn in South Africa, people of all races voted in the country's first fully democratic election. They elected as their president the leader of the African National Congress, Nelson Mandela.

The people of South Africa queued for many hours on polling day, anxious to be able to cast their vote and be a part of history in the making.

Nelson Mandela had been the world's most famous prisoner for 27 years before he was released in 1990 and his political party, the ANC, was legalized. He had been sent to gaol for life in 1962 for leading armed opposition against the apartheid regime.

Nelson Mandela casts his vote for the ANC in the first all-race elections in South Africa on 27 April 1994.

President Mandela's election was a symbol of a new beginning in a new South Africa where citizens of all races now

'give all South Africans their full human rights'

have equal rights. But South Africa's problems did not come to an end when a black president took office. Apartheid has left a legacy of poverty for the black majority. They want, above all, jobs, better housing and high quality education for their children: the basic human rights spelt out in the Universal Declaration.

Mandela's message to the wealthy countries of the West is: help us to build a South Africa which is not only democratic and free, but can also afford to give all its people a share in prosperity. Help us to give all South Africans their full human rights.

People's rights 3839
still at risk

Bringing about change in South Africa was a great victory for peaceful negotiations. There have been changes elsewhere, too. Since the end of Communist control between 1989-1991, new democracies have sprung up in Eastern Europe. For the first time in generations people in Russia can now vote freely for their parliament and their president. Democracy has been restored in many of the countries previously controlled by

In Bucharest, the capital of Romania, workmen dismantle the statue of Lenin, symbol of the Communist dictatorship there, after its defeat in 1991.

Children light candles in Prague, Czechoslovakia, to celebrate the anniversary of the 'Velvet Revolution' in 1989 which led to the peaceful overthrow of Communism.

Communist dictatorships, where people had not been able to exercise their right to vote freely, such as Poland, Hungary and the former Czechoslovakia. Small countries which had been completely absorbed by their bigger neighbours, like Latvia and Estonia, have become independent.

But many countries are still ruled by tyrannical

'many countries are still ruled by tyrannical governments'

governments. Their human rights are still being violated, often cruelly. In Iraq, Saddam Hussein is still in control in spite of the Gulf War in which his army was defeated. China still controls Tibet, which it took by force, and where it is trying to eliminate the unique Tibetan culture. Indonesia has killed hundreds of thousands of people in East Timor, which it invaded and took over twenty years ago.

Place: East Timor
Time: October 1996
The Issue: Freedom for small nations

The Nobel Peace Prize for 1996 was awarded to Bishop Belo and Jose Ramos-Horta. They are two leaders of a long campaign for justice and human rights in the tiny country of East Timor which was taken over by its larger neighbour, Indonesia, in 1975.

On ten occasions the United Nations has asked Indonesia to withdraw and allow the people of East Timor to decide their own future. They have been ignored. Only a few Western journalists and campaigners have reminded governments over the years of the illegal occupation that some would rather forget. It is estimated that over 200,000 people, a third of the population, were either killed or died of starvation in the early years of Indonesia's occupation of East Timor.

In 1991, 200 young people in a peaceful funeral procession were shot dead by Indonesian troops in a cemetery in East Timor.

(Above right) The Roman Catholic bishop, Carlos Belo, and resistance leader Jose Ramos-Horta, accept the Nobel Peace Prize for their part in the struggle against the Indonesian occupation of East Timor.

(Right) Timorese students lie dead and wounded in the Santa Cruz cemetery. The shootings by the Indonesian troops were captured on film and shown all around the world.

Torture

Governments still persecute people for their religious or political beliefs or because they oppose the people who hold power. Article 5 of the Universal Declaration of Human Rights outlaws torture and inhuman and degrading treatment, but it is one of the reasons why refugees flee from one country to another.

In East Timor, opponents of the Indonesian regime are regularly detained and tortured and sometimes killed. In Indonesia, too, supporters of East Timor have been injured or killed by police and soldiers in recent years.

'international pressure'

In an effort to limit these human rights abuses, countries sometimes try to use the power of international pressure. The United States, for example, has banned the export of crowd control equipment and armoured vehicles which have been used against unarmed Indonesian protesters, causing death and serious injury. Indonesia's own Human Rights Commission has criticized the use of armoured vehicles against protesters. Amnesty International is trying to persuade the British government to stop the sale of similar equipment to Indonesia by a British firm.

Police pull a victim to safety after an attack on the Indonesian consulate in Amsterdam: part of the violence surrounding the struggle for independence in East Timor. Just as East Timor wants independence, prior to 1949 Indonesia strove for its freedom from the Dutch.

Pressure and persistence

Individual businesses have also responded to this type of pressure from human rights groups, the public and investors who hold shares (small parts of the business). For example, the Dutch beer producers, Heineken, abandoned plans to build a new brewery in Myanmar (Burma) when they were put under pressure by those who disagreed with the military regime there. SLORC (State Law and Order Restoration Council), the military dictators of Myanmar, would not accept the results of a free, democratic election held in 1990. They took control of the country for themselves.

The leader of the opposition party and true winner of the elections, Aung San Suu Kyi, was kept under house arrest for six years. Human rights supporters were delighted that their protests succeeded in persuading a company such as Heineken to abandon its plans.

Finally freed from house arrest, Aung San Suu Kyi holds a rally outside her home.

Such pressure, and the pressure of each nation upon its neighbour, is one way to help prevent inequalities and human rights violations from continuing. But the pressure has to be maintained in order to be effective. It took a great deal of persistence, and action by governments as well as individuals, to defeat apartheid. But in the end it was defeated. That must give hope to anyone who suffers injustice anywhere and everyone who campaigns against injustice everywhere.

British parliamentarians celebrate Aung San Suu Kyi's 50th birthday as part of Amnesty International's campaign against her prolonged house arrest.

EQUAL OPPORTUNITIES

Date:
September 1996
Place:
Tuzla, Bosnia-Hercegovina
The issue:
Equal opportunities, regardless of religion or political belief

Liljiana Vesovic is a Muslim married to a Christian Serb. In Bosnia this is a difficult position to find yourself in at the end of a terrible civil war between the three different communities who live in this part of former Yugoslavia. But throughout four years of war stretching from 1992 to 1995, the town of Tuzla was a place where the three groups, Muslims, Croats and Serbs, lived in relative harmony.

But after the peace agreement, when free elections were held for a new Bosnian government, harmony in Tuzla came to an end and discrimination began. Liljiana was director of a detergent factory in Tuzla at a time when the mainly Muslim Party for Democratic Action was taking control of the town.

When Liljiana refused to join the party she was sacked. When she refused to give up her job, party members changed the lock on her office door so that she could not return to work. The chances of the three ethnic groups continuing to work together in Tuzla started to look increasingly slim. Liljiana was not the only individual being bullied into doing as she was told by the politicians.

The Bosnian Serb leader, Radovan Karadzic (right), and his military commander, General Ratko Mladic (left), have been accused of serious human rights abuses in the UN International War Crimes Tribunal. The political situation that has developed in the former Yugoslavia has created a difficult atmosphere in which to live and work.

Discrimination and the right to work

There were no laws to say that Liljiana Vesovic should lose her job. But because she would not do as she was told, local politicians took the law into their own hands and made sure that she could not work because of who she was and what she believed in. She was punished simply for being a Muslim married to a Serb, and for refusing to be bullied about her politics.

'Equal treatment is a basic human right'

If people like Liljiana Vesovic are kept out of jobs through discrimination, they lose their right to earn money to support themselves and their families. Article 23 of the Universal Declaration of Human Rights says that everyone has the right to work, the right to free choice of employment, to decent conditions and to protection from unemployment regardless of race or religion or any other difference. The right to equal treatment is a basic human right.

Young people looking for jobs have the right not to be turned down because of differences in race, religion or gender.

The right to earn a living is important, not only for people's dignity, but also simply to enable them to support themselves and their families, regardless of who they are.

Equal opportunities

Equal opportunity is an important human right – every individual should have the same access to education and jobs no matter what their background. The right to work is a crucial way of helping people to escape poverty and live their lives in comfort and security. There are many reasons why people are unable to find work, but in many countries discrimination is still a significant one.

Date: 1996
Place:
Denmark
The Issue:
The right name
for the job

Alica Lajtner lives in Denmark. She is half Danish and half Bosnian. When she left college she applied for a job with a well-respected Danish company and was told that she would hear from them within a month. When she had not heard after two months she went along in person to try to find out what had happened.

'foreign-sounding
name'

On the manager's desk she saw two piles of applications. One contained all those from applicants with Danish names, the other all those from people with foreign-sounding names. Alica's application was in the 'foreign' pile. The manager seemed surprised that she had blond hair and blue eyes – a typical 'Dane' with a foreign name. 'This made me realize that you can come across discrimination even in well-respected companies which are supposed to have an intelligent workforce,' Alica said.

Ability or background?

It is not only governments which discriminate. In day-to-day life, even in countries which claim all their citizens are equal, it is individuals who make decisions about jobs. They can make a nonsense of equality.

According to Census data collected in the UK in 1991, workers from ethnic minorities experienced higher rates of unemployment than white workers. When they found jobs they tended to be in less skilled occupations than white people. People of Bangladeshi origin in the UK found it four times harder to get work than the white population.

In many countries, workers from minority groups often find that the only jobs available to them are the low-skilled, poorly paid jobs that no one else wants.

Looking for work

This trend is similar in many other European countries which have ethnic minority groups, such as the Netherlands, France and Germany. In these countries, research shows that school-leavers from ethnic minority groups looking for a job have more difficulty finding work than their white class-mates even when they have the same examination results. The same is true in the United States where African-American families earn on average about three-fifths of what white families earn because they work in the most poorly paid jobs and are more likely to be unemployed.

'Untouchable' women, *dalits*, are still at the bottom of the social scale in India.

Date: 1996
Place: India
The issue:
No equal rights for the poorest of the poor

Research shows that ethnic minorities in Europe and the US often find it more difficult to find work after leaving school.

In India, governments have tried for most of this century to give equal rights to people known as the Untouchables. The Hindu religion divides people into social groups, or castes, according to the work they do; the Untouchables were only allowed to do the dirtiest jobs. It has been very difficult to overcome this tradition. Mahatma Ghandi, the leader who fought peacefully for Indian independence from British rule, renamed the Untouchables *Harijans*, or People of God. Schools and colleges were set up especially for them and jobs reserved for them so that they could play a full part in society.

Equal access – except if you are poor

Sometimes people do not have to be of a different race to be discriminated against. Being poor is enough. If you live in a certain area which is known for poverty and crime, it will be hard to find a job, borrow money or buy a better house.

Poverty can be a vicious circle. Without a home and address it is difficult to get a job, without a job, it is hard to afford a home.

The power of tradition

In some countries tradition may be much stronger than laws which say that people must be treated equally. Religion or social customs may dictate that some people should be treated differently when it comes to finding jobs and earning a living for their families.

'the poorest in a poor country'

This has indeed been the case in India. Even by the late 1990s, the *Harijans* remained among the poorest in a poor country. Although discrimination has not been stopped, more and more young people in India are rejecting tradition. They are opposing discrimination which prevents the poorest people ever having the chance to improve themselves by getting good jobs. Even when discrimination is made illegal, as it is in India, the United States and most Western countries, it still goes on.

(Above) Even in Germany, which now has strict laws to prevent a repetition of its Nazi past, there are groups attempting to revive the prejudice and hatred of the Nazi era.

The slave markets of Africa sent millions of Africans across the Atlantic to work in captivity.

The civil rights movement

Dealing with discrimination and fighting for equal rights is an on-going challenge. Slaves in America and the West Indies had to fight for their right to live and work as free citizens; women in most countries have had to struggle to gain the vote and equal pay, and for some the struggle continues; Roman Catholics were denied civil rights in Ireland and the UK for hundreds of years. Many governments or peoples still deny rights to those who have little power.

Dr Martin Luther King, Jr won the Nobel Peace Prize for his inspired leadership of the non-violent campaign for civil rights for black people in the United States between 1955 and 1968. He was assassinated in 1968.

The Ku Klux Klan is a secret society of racist whites who terrorize fellow black citizens in the southern states of the US.

The 13th, 14th and 15th amendments to the American Constitution (1865-1870) made the black people of America free and equal American citizens, in theory. However, they still suffered the most appalling discrimination, particularly in the southern states. By 1957, Dr Martin Luther King, Jr became the figurehead of the modern Civil Rights Movement, arousing much national support against the continued segregation and second-class treatment of black people. The struggle continued and by the early 1970s laws such as the Equal Employment Opportunities Act (1972) signalled that at last some progress was being made.

Redressing the balance

However, proving discrimination is not easy. It is one thing to know that a whole group of people is being treated unfairly – you can count up how many are unemployed, you can discover what they earn, you can find out where they live. It is much harder to prove that when school-leavers apply for a job in a local factory, shop or office they have been turned down because they are black, or gypsies or Jews.

A column of 5000 civil rights protesters, led by Dr Martin Luther King, Jr, march through Selma, Alabama, in 1965.

Positive discrimination

There are different ways of dealing with this problem. The approach in the United States has been to insist that different groups are represented in jobs in the same proportion that they are represented in the population of a city or a state. For instance, if half the population of Georgia is African-American, then it is expected that half the jobs in the police force, the schools or the state offices should be taken by African-American citizens. This is called positive discrimination, or affirmative action, and it has led to a big increase in the number of black Americans going to university and gaining professional jobs.

(Left) Though some young black people still face discrimination in the way they are treated at school or when they apply for jobs, many countries now have equal opportunities legislation. This was brought in to ensure that all the ethnic and cultural minorities that make up different societies have equal access to education and so the possibility of getting a good job.

(Below) The report 'The Tottenham Experiment' shows that in the UK young black people are twice as likely to be stopped or arrested by the police than whites. Part of the reason given for these arrests was that in 81% of street robberies, victims claimed their attackers were black.

eing treated fairly'

Equal access, equal treatment

But equal rights is about being treated fairly and equally, about equal access and equal opportunities. Is it right, then, that some people should get jobs or university places simply because of the colour of their skin, or the fact that they are women, rather than because they are well qualified for what they want to do? In the United States there is now a political divide between those who feel that positive discrimination has helped minorities and women, and that it is still needed, and those who feel that it is making it harder for others, often white men, who are equally well qualified, to get a decent education and good jobs.

Equal but not the same

But equal rights do not necessarily mean treating people in exactly the same way. Perhaps there are instances when a group that has been discriminated against for many years needs additional help for a certain period of time in order to overcome the obstacles that have been put in its way? Perhaps when there are more women, or people from different ethnic backgrounds, in positions where they can help themselves, these special conditions will no longer be needed?

The violation of rights of different groups of people, such as the African Americans in the southern states of the US, shows that tools such as positive discrimination are perhaps needed to redress the balance.

Helping to help themselves

Many people who belong to groups who have been discriminated against feel that in order to influence their own future they need to be much more active in representing themselves, just as Steve Biko felt that black people should become involved in fighting for their own rights. Indeed, women across the nations of the world have been moved to stand up for what they believe to be their rights.

In democratic countries the police are seen as being important for protecting civil rights. Some groups, however, feel that the police take away their rights. The police often face difficult situations; they must calm heated exchanges between different ethnic groups.

Date: 1996
Place: Sweden
The issue: The right to be a mother and go out to work

Gunnel Danielson is a reporter for a Swedish newspaper. She has a baby son, Peter, who is looked after at a child-care centre when she and her partner, Sven, are both at work in the afternoons. 'I'm at home in the mornings to look after Peter and Sven is at home in the evenings. It is good that there are times when Sven and Peter do things together. Peter and I do other things.' In Sweden both parents can share the period of parental leave which follows the birth of a baby. When they go back to work there are well-staffed day-care centres available until children go to school. After school children can be looked after in special centres until their parents come home from work.

It is not always easy for people to take advantage of their rights. Very few countries deny mothers with young children the right to work. But going to work may be impossible if there is no child-care available.

The right to work and child-care

The rights which working women like Gunnel Danielson now enjoy in Sweden only came after a long struggle. Even now, many Western countries discriminate against women in many ways. It is hard, for instance, to go to work and earn a living once you have become a mother unless you can make arrangements to have your child well looked after while you are at work.

'poorly paid and less secure'

Returning to work

Many mothers who return to work often take part-time jobs so that they can care for their children after school. However, part-time work is often poorly paid and less secure than a full time post.

Some mothers, however, are not in a position to argue with their employers about the working conditions – they have to take what is available.

One-parent families

Good child-care is even more crucial for one-parent families. A survey in 1996 showed that in countries where child-care for single mothers is either free, such as France and Belgium, or very cheap, as in Denmark and Sweden, far more single mothers took jobs. Where child-care is expensive, as in the UK, the majority of single mothers depend on welfare benefits – money provided by the taxpayer and paid by the state.

The level of child-care is important for any parent who has to leave his or her child when they go out to work.

Few legal rights

The difficulties that women face in the workplace in the 1990s, in education, employment and civil rights, have changed over the last century. Indeed, at the beginning of the twentieth century women in the Western world were often not allowed to work at all and had very few legal rights generally.

For many centuries laws were based upon a view of women which regarded them as subordinate, or inferior and answerable, to men. Women were denied political rights and rights to their own property. Any possessions or fortunes became the property of their husbands when they married. Similarly, family names inherited from their fathers were usually changed to their husbands' name on marriage. Women could not inherit their fathers' estates or title if there was a male relative to do so. Even now, in the UK, a king or queen is still only succeeded by his or her daughter if there is no son to inherit the title.

Daughters may be treated the same as sons in many respects, but not if they are the children of royalty, like the Belgian Royal Family shown here. Most monarchies still follow the tradition of passing the crown to the eldest son.

Many of the crowd on Derby Day look to see the result of the race, unaware of the drama unfolding in front of them, as Emily Davison falls beneath the King's horse.

Date: 4 June 1913
Place: Epsom, UK
The issue: Fighting for the right to be equal

Emily Davison had many clashes with the law in the UK. In her bid to win the vote for women she had often been imprisoned and gone on hunger strikes to bring publicity to her cause. In a suffragette protest she ran onto the course of the Derby horse race at Epsom on 4 June 1913. She fell under the King's horse and was trampled. She died four days later.

Thousands of suffragettes attended the funeral procession through the streets of London and Emily Davison became a martyr, a figurehead who died for the suffragette cause.

'upholding their right to vote'

The liberation of women

One of the most dramatic and least violent battles for equal rights took place in the Western democracies at the end of the nineteenth century. Women like Emily Davison, known as suffragettes, began to fight for their rights, including their right to vote. Women's movements went on to claim their rights to education, training and the right to work.

Men were reluctant to share their status, wealth and power with women, which meant that women's bid for equal rights really had to be fought for. One of the most important campaigns was for women to gain the vote. Without being able to vote for someone to represent them in government, women did not believe that anyone would take them or their beliefs seriously. To achieve real equality, laws would have to be changed.

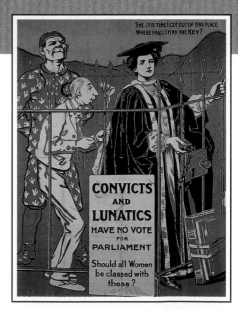

As part of their campaign, suffragettes protested about women being grouped with 'convicts and lunatics' (the mentally ill) who were also excluded from voting.

The right to vote

The first country to give women the vote was New Zealand in 1893, quickly followed by Australia and many of the European democracies. In 1920, women were given the vote in the United States and the UK. In Switzerland, however, women did not win the right to vote until 1971 after a national referendum, when the issue was put to the country to decide. But women can now vote virtually everywhere in the world, except for a few Muslim countries.

Elizabeth Garrett Anderson

Date: 1865
Place: Edinburgh, Scotland
The Issue: The right of a woman to decide on her own future

In Victorian England, when young Elizabeth Garrett Anderson decided that she wanted to become a doctor, there was no university or hospital that would train her because she was a woman. But Elizabeth was very determined. She persuaded some male doctors to teach her privately and gained some more experience in London hospitals. She then went to Scotland in 1895 where she was granted a licence to practise medicine legally. She was the first woman to qualify as a doctor in the UK. Dr Garrett Anderson and her colleagues eventually persuaded all the universities and hospitals in the UK to open their doors to women students of medicine.

Women voters were seen as important participants in the 1996 US elections.

Winning acceptance

Women have also faced a long struggle in the workplace. The idea that a young woman like Elizabeth Garrett Anderson should become a doctor, able to examine and treat men as well as women, was regarded as quite scandalous in her lifetime.

'There was a change in attitudes'

There was a big change in attitudes after the First World War, when women had been welcomed as essential workers in factories, as nurses at the

battle front, and in many jobs previously regarded as men-only. In 1919 in the UK, it was made illegal to prevent women from holding public office or from entering professional jobs like medicine and the law. But this did not mean it was easy for women to find jobs or to be elected to public office.

Discrimination still occurred. Between the wars it was very common for women to be asked to leave their jobs when they married. It was believed that a married woman's place was at home looking after her husband and children.

Equality in the workplace

After the Second World War equal pay for women became an issue in most Western countries. Before that women were paid less than men even if they were doing exactly the same job. Gradually the democracies began to change their laws in response to women's demands and protests in each country. In 1963, for example, the Federal Equal Pay Act in the US made it illegal to pay women a different wage from men for doing the same work. In the UK, the Equal Pay Act was passed in 1970.

In the Second World War, thousands of women took on jobs as part of the war effort in both the US and the UK.

Today, women are usually entitled to 'equal pay for work of equal value' – so that different jobs could be assessed to evaluate their worth. For instance, the job of a skilled, generally male, technician might be compared to that of a skilled, generally female, secretary, to fix a fair wage for both. In the European Union this is a right guaranteed in all the member states by EU laws.

The 'glass ceiling'

But, in spite of these laws, discrimination is difficult to prove. Some bosses still feel women are not suitable for senior jobs. The

barrier which women sometimes find prevents them from gaining promotion to top jobs is known as the 'glass ceiling'. It occurs when women who have reached a certain level in a company and are keen to progress are not promoted to management positions purely because of their sex. Insignificant problems are put in their way, purely to prevent their success, keeping all the women in that company below a certain level. This invisible barrier creates a 'glass ceiling'.

As more opportunities open up, women have taken on roles that once they would not even have considered. Gro Harlem Brundtland first became Prime Minister of Norway in 1981.

Where discrimination in the workplace has occurred and can be proved, some women have successfully taken their cases to court to win their rights. In Europe in the 1970s, a Belgian woman challenged the fact that she had to retire at the age of 40 as a airline hostess, when male stewards did not. The case led to the court amending European legislation to ensure a right for equal pay and equal treatment in employment and training.

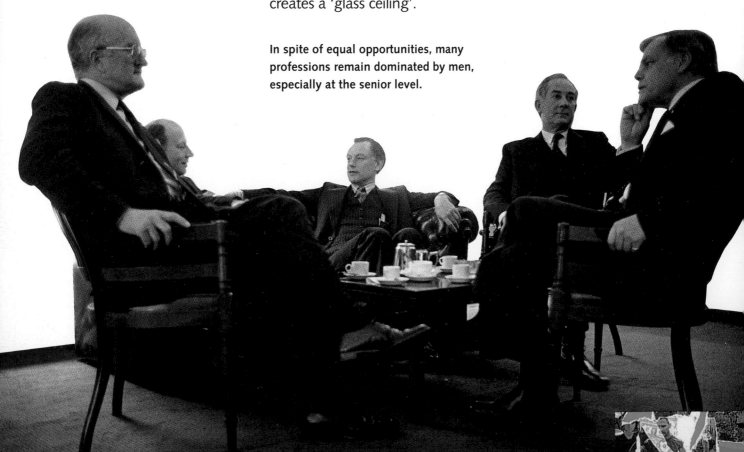

In spite of equal opportunities, many professions remain dominated by men, especially at the senior level.

Date:1996
Place:Afghanistan
Issue: The right of women
to learn and work

Since the Muslim fundamentalist soldiers called the Taliban took over the capital city, Kabul, Safia has not been able to go to her job working for a relief agency and her mother, a primary school teacher, has also had to stay at home. The new rulers in Kabul have begun a campaign to force the people to live by the Taliban's strict interpretation of Islamic law. They have banned television and music as an evil influence.

'Men and women should be equal under Islam'

But those who are suffering most under this harsh new regime are women. They have been forced into traditional dress and all girls' schools and colleges have been closed. Women are no longer allowed to work, ride bicycles or drive cars. If they walk in the street they must be accompanied by a male relative and dress in a burka which covers them from head to foot. Women who do not comply risk being whipped by the soldiers.

Many women in Kabul hate the new laws. 'Men and women should be equal under Islam,' Safia says.

Even among Muslims there is dispute about the Taliban's very strict interpretation of women's role. Some leading Muslim scholars argue that the Koran should not be interpreted in a way which denies women the right to study or work, or move about freely.

A cultural difference

In many countries the treatment of women is still based on traditional, and often religious, ideas of what women may and may not do. This is particularly so in rural communities.

The price of being female

In some cultures girls are still seen very much as the property of their fathers, or of their husbands when they marry. They often do not have a choice about whom they may marry, and can be married off at a very young age. Once they are married they may be regarded by their husband's family as a sort of slave. In extreme cases, young wives in India, for example, have been murdered by the husbands' family because their dowries (a fee paid on marriage by the bride's family) is too small or the women do not go on to produce children.

Dowries have been made illegal in India, but the custom is still observed by some.

Baby girls are often regarded as a burden in countries such as India, not only because of the cost of paying dowries, but because daughters cannot earn as much as sons. Elderly parents rely on the income of their children as there is no state benefit. But boys are usually educated in preference to girls. In India, 65% of boys over the age of 15 are able to read compared with 38% of girls, so men are usually able to get better jobs than women.

In China, where couples are officially allowed only one child, baby girls are often abandoned or put into state orphanages. Sons are seen as much more valuable.

Women and girls in Iran are harrassed if they do not wear the traditional chador which covers them from head to toe. In Saudi Arabia, women are not permitted to drive cars. There are strict rules regarding whom they may go out with in public. Is it impossible for traditions, central to a culture, to be observed without violating women's rights? Perhaps the validity of each tradition needs to be reassessed?

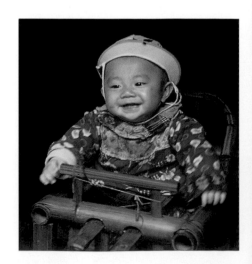

**Time:
October 1996
Place:
Kuwait
The issue:
The right to
vote**

Men and women in
Kuwait, the only Gulf
State which has an
elected parliament,
demonstrate to
demand political rights
for women. Kuwaiti
women have more
freedom than many

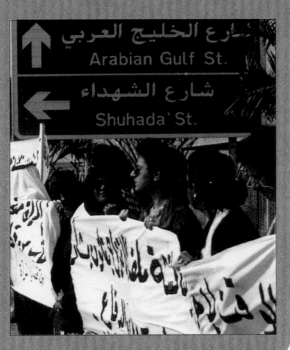

These women in Kuwait believe that they can be both good Muslim citizens and have the right to vote.

Arab women. They work in business, the civil service and the oil
industry. But they have been told that they must wait until the next
century before they are allowed to take part in elections. At present
they cannot stand for parliament or vote.

A promise

Although some women in
developing countries have the
right to vote, such as in Pakistan
where from 1988 until 1996 the
country twice voted in a woman
prime minister, the fight for the
right of women to vote has not
been won all over the world. In
1996 women in the Arab state of
Kuwait demonstrated for the
right to vote which had been
promised to them – but not until
the year 2000.

A way forward

Education is seen as a key tool in
addressing the equal opportunites
issue across the world.
Governments and women's
groups are working to make sure
that girls in developing countries
get the same education and
training as boys. Only this sort of
progress will allow them to take
an equal place in the societies in
which they live.

Ability to read and write, in percentages, of people over 15 years of age, in 1995

	males	females
Afghanistan	47	15
India	65	38
South Africa	82	82
China	90	73
Saudi Arabia	72	50
United States	99*	99*

Figures from 1997 State of the World's
Children (*data may not refer to year in table
heading or refer to only part of the country)

In Afghanistan, between 1990-1995, the
number of boys enrolled for primary school
was 42% compared to only 14% of girls.

Many children with disabilities lead happy lives with their families and at school. But sometimes they find that they do not have the same rights as everyone else.

Date:
1996
Place:
London, UK
The issue:
An equal right to medical treatment

Amanda Richards is nine years old and she has a hole in her heart. Over the years this has affected her ability to breathe properly and even just walking up the stairs makes her breathless. Her lungs are now so badly damaged that she needs a heart and lung transplant if she is to live much longer. But the specialist doctors at a hospital famous for its success with such operations will not recommend Amanda for the transplant.

Organs which can be transplanted are scarce and people with disabilities are not put on the waiting list. Amanda has Down's Syndrome – a genetic condition which results in some mental disability and sometimes results in early death. The hospital's policy affects anyone with any disability. When faced with the difficult choice of who should get scarce replacement organs, the hospital gives priority to the person who is most 'normal'. Amanda is a normal youngster in many ways. She goes to the local middle school, she likes swimming, eating spare ribs and going to parties. But soon she will die, because in one crucial way she is different. She is mentally disabled. There will be no transplant operation to save her life.

'normal'

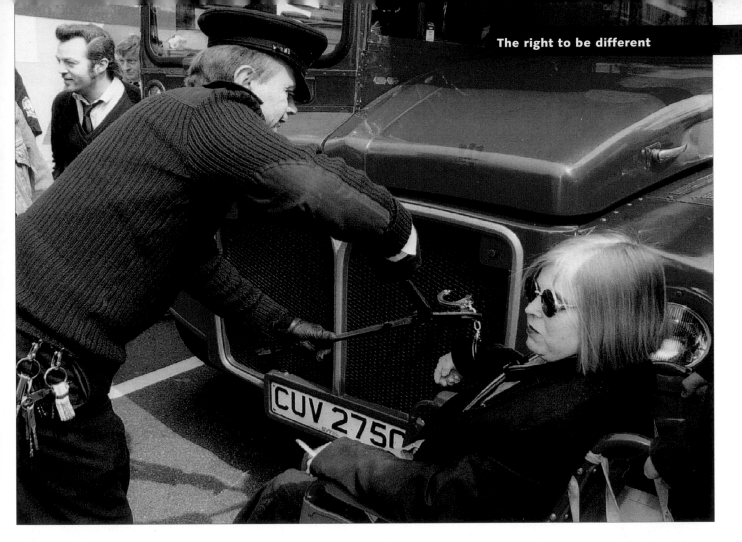

In a bid to get the right access to public transport for people with disabilities, a frustrated group of protesters chained themselves to London buses in 1995.

Being different

The most common forms of discrimination are on the grounds of race, religion or gender. But there are all sorts of other reasons why one group of people may be singled out for unfair treatment by other groups. People with disabilities have to fight hard for equal treatment. Because they are a minority and their needs can be very specific, many governments are reluctant to address their bid to be treated equally and fairly, as it often proves costly to do so.

Many of us are used to the wheelchair sign indicating ramps and doors for disabled people, but there is no law which says public transport must be accessible to all. Having got to the bus stop or train station, it is impossible for some people, those in wheelchairs for example, to board the bus or train.

Finding a job as a disabled person is often very hard, even though some Western countries have introduced positive discrimination.

Many employers say they do not have the facilities to cater for certain types of disability and claim that doing so would create

'transport must be accessible to all'

a health and safety risk. To rectify this, legislation has been brought in since the mid-1970s in many Western countries specifying that any new building should be planned and built with disabled access and provision for people with disabilities in mind.

A sexual preference

People who are homosexual (sexually attracted to people of the same sex) often face prejudice and discrimination. Like the Jewish people in Nazi Germany, homosexual people were also persecuted, with over 100,000 being sent to die in the Nazi concentration camps. In the streets of Europe, America and Australia, homosexuals are still at risk of being attacked and mugged, simply because of their sexuality. In Iran, Mauritania and some other Islamic states, homosexual acts are still punishable by execution.

'at risk of being attacked and mugged'

In terms of employment, in many Western countries equal opportunities laws apply to homosexual people, but again, it is not always easy to uncover discrimination. In Britain, in 1997, however, the debate about admitting homosexual men and women into the armed forces openly continued. Those against their inclusion said they could affect the way the forces performed their duties. Other Western countries, including Australia, the Netherlands and the United States, do not have such restrictions and permit gay and lesbian recruits.

This group of gay and lesbian officers took legal action to get the ban lifted on homosexuals serving in the British armed forces. In some countries discrimination against gay military personnel is illegal.

In the United States, the Constitution outlaws discrimination on the grounds of age. Many older people in the US take advantage of the fact that they can go on working long after the official retirement age.

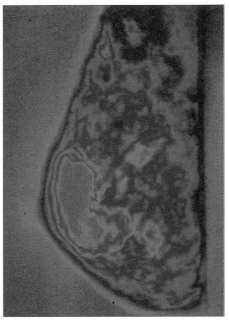

X-ray screening to detect breast cancer is important, but it may not always be available to those who need it the most.

'Only the under-forties need apply'

Age is another excuse for discrimination. Many companies set age limits for certain jobs, making it very difficult for someone who loses a job in their forties or fifties to find another. In the United States age discrimination in jobs is illegal and people are able to work on into their late sixties and seventies if they feel able to do so.

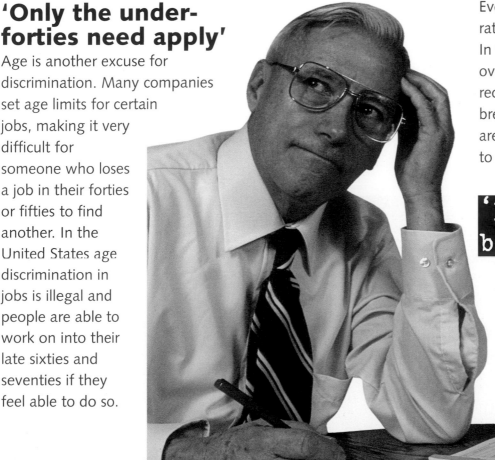

Even health care may be rationed on the grounds of age. In the UK, for example, women over the age of 65 are not recommended for screening for breast cancer, even though they are in the age-group most likely to contract the disease.

'health care may be rationed'

Treatment for heart disease may also be refused to older people because doctors believe it is not worth spending the money on the elderly.

41

On a smaller scale, something like the Holocaust has happened again and again around the world in the last fifty years: in East Timor, in Myanmar (Burma), in Iraq, in parts of Africa. But the horror and outrage felt by the nations of the world over the Holocaust resulted in countries trying to cooperate to prevent such atrocities from ever happening again. It was such cooperation that helped break down apartheid in South Africa.

Years of protest

It took many years of protest, and many deaths to overcome apartheid in South Africa and to win equality for blacks in America. Those campaigns were won, and though there are many more to fight before human rights become a reality for many of the people of the world, the same tools that have been successful in the past can be used again.

On a more individual scale, new help is now available in the fight for human rights. In Europe, for example, the European Court of Human Rights has challenged some countries to amend, create or uphold legislation in a bid to uphold human rights. These include issues relating to equal work for equal pay and the rights of gay men and lesbians for homosexual equality.

This picture, transmitted digitally, captures the drama of the moment as a single Chinese citizen stands in front of a convoy of tanks. He formed part of a mass student protest for human rights in Tiananmen Square, Beijing, on 4 June 1989.

The joy of the first all-races, democratic election in South Africa shows what can be achieved when countries work together to uphold human rights.

A fight worth fighting

The Universal Declaration of Human Rights is not a set of laws which countries have to obey. It is a set of principles that all members of the United Nations are expected to observe. A whole range of international human rights conventions have developed from the UDHR. Once a government has agreed to be bound by the UDHR, it has to change its own domestic laws to fit in with what is laid down in the Declaration. Some governments do so willingly, some have to be persuaded to do so, and some still violate human rights in the cruellest ways.

'a set of principles'

But history tells us that people and governments can be persuaded to change. The United Nations, national governments, political parties, businesses and charities can help bring about change for the better. And so can individuals.

Even on our own doorsteps we can make a difference. Every one of us can resist the temptation to discriminate

The United Nations, with its headquarters in New York, has had its problems and is desperately short of money, but it has succeeded in many of its humanitarian projects.

against people who are different in some way. Everyone can protest when they see someone else being hurt by unfairness and injustice. Human rights are not something which only concern people in far-away places. They start in our own community, with our own neighbours. And the battle against prejudice and injustice can be won.

43

GLOSSARY

apartheid: the system of government in South Africa which separated the different racial groups in the population, giving only the white population full rights of citizenship.

assassinate: to murder an important figure, for example, a president or monarch, often for political reasons.

burka: a garment worn by women that covers the whole body and includes a veiled piece for the eyes.

chador: the head and body covering or scarf often worn by Muslim and Hindu women and girls to cover themselves.

civil rights: a set of basic rights aimed at protecting the citizens of a country.

civil war: war within the boundaries of a country between the fellow citizens of that country.

coma: a state of deep unconsciousness.

Communism: Communism is based on the political views outlined in the writings of Karl Marx. It upholds the view that the state, not private individuals, should control industry and agriculture, in order to create a more equal society where wealth is divided as fairly as possible.

concentration camp: prison and work camps established by the Nazis where millions of people either died, due to the horrific conditions, or were killed.

conscience: the sense of right and wrong which influences how people behave.

culture: the shared beliefs and way of life of a particular group of people.

democratic: involving everyone in decision-making, about how a country is run, usually by voting for parliamentary representatives at elections.

dictatorship: a country run by a leader who holds complete power.

discrimination: treating a person or a group of people less favourably than another person or group on the gounds of their race, religion, gender or other difference.

economy (economic): all the activities concerned with the buying and selling of goods and services.

elite: a group of people at the top of an organization or country.

ethnic: belonging to one distinct racial or national group of people.

fundamentalist: someone who believes in absolute basic principles, often used to describe religious extremists.

ghetto: originally the separate areas of towns to which Jews were confined, but in modern times used to describe areas where a minority group lives apart from the majority – generally a poor area of town.

Holocaust: the murder by the Nazis of 11 million civilians, including six million European Jews, in death camps during the Second World War. Victims also included gypsies, homosexuals and the mentally ill.

homosexual: a person who is attracted to people of the same, rather than the opposite, sex.

inauguration: a formal ceremony, in this instance acknowledging Nelson Mandela as the new President of South Africa.

injustice: an unjust, or unfair action.

Koran: the holy book, or Muslim Scriptures, containing the word of God as spoken by the Islamic Prophet, Mohammed.

legacy: in the context of this book, a code of behaviour or a set of traditions absorbed over many years into a country's culture.

military regime: a government, usually unelected, run by the armed forces.

minorities: groups living in a society who are not of the same race, culture or religion as the majority group.

Nazi: a supporter of the National Socialist Party, led by Adolf Hitler, in Germany before and during the Second World War.

origin: the beginning of something, or, for people, their ancestry or birthplace.

persecuted: picked on and tormented.

persistence: a determination to continue a course of action.

positive discrimination: giving extra consideration or help to people who may have suffered discrimination.

prejudice: literally means to prejudge something. If you are prejudiced against something, it means that you have an unreasonable dislike of it without even having found out about it, or thought it through properly.

privileged: someone has had a privileged upbringing if, for example, they have had more advantages in life than others.

prosperity: financial, or monetary wealth.

quota: fixed number or amount; for example, governments may require certain quotas of women or ethnic minorities to be employed by businesses in an effort to redress equal opportunities' problems.

referendum: a vote asking every citizen of a country to decide on a particular issue.

refugees: people who have fled to another country to escape persecution.

republic: a country which has a president as head of state.

safe haven: in the context of this book, the areas set up in Iraq where Kurds fleeing from Saddam Hussein and his army were protected by the United Nations troops.

sanctions: when one country stops the sale or purchase of products to or from another country in order to pressurize that country into changing a policy or course of action.

segregation: the enforced separation of groups of people by law or by custom.

tyrannical: tyrannical use of power is when a position of power is abused and people are governed by threats and through fear.

vicious circle: when one negative event leads on to another making it hard for someone caught up in the situation to break free. They may think things will never go right for them again.

violate: in this book, to disregard or break an agreement, or code of behaviour.

welfare benefits: payments made by the state to help people who are in difficulties, such as unemployment or ill health.

USEFUL ADDRESSES

Amnesty International, UK
99 Rosebery Avenue
LONDON
EC1 4RE
Tel: 0171 814 6200

Amnesty International
Australian Section
134 Broadway Road
Broadway
SYDNEY
AUSTRALIA
Tel: 61 2 9281 4188

Antislavery International
Stable Yard
Broomgrove Road
LONDON SW9 1TL
Tel: 0171 924 9555

Australian Red Cross
Red Cross House
159 Clarence Street
SYDNEY
NSW 2000
AUSTRALIA
Tel: 61 2 9229 4111

Civil Liberties Trust
21 Tabard Street
LONDON SE1 4LA
Tel: 0171 403 3888

Commission for Racial Equality
Elliot House
10-12 Allington Street
LONDON
SW1E 5EH
Tel: 0171 828 7022

Equal Opportunities Commission
Overseas House
Quay Street
MANCHESTER M3 3HN
Tel: 0161 833 9244

Equal Opportunities Tribunal
ADC House
99 Elizabeth Street
SYDNEY NSW 2000
AUSTRALIA
Tel: 61 2 9231 2911

Industrial Relations of NSW
Level 9, Xerox House
815-825a George Street
SYDNEY NSW 2000
AUSTRALIA
Tel: 61 2 9288 8600

INDEX

Radbrook LRC